SPORTING CHAMPIONSHIPS
WORLD SERIES

Alan Cho

W

WEIGL PUBLISHERS INC.

Published by Weigl Publishers Inc.
350 5th Avenue, Suite 3304, PMB 6G
New York, NY 10118-0069

Website: www.weigl.com

Library of Congress Cataloging-in-Publication Data

Cho, Alan.
 World series / Alan Cho.
     p. cm. -- (Sporting championships)
 Includes index.
 ISBN 978-1-59036-699-8 (hard cover : alk. paper) -- ISBN 978-1-59036-700-1 (soft cover : alk. paper)
 1. World Series (Baseball)--Juvenile literature. 2. Baseball--United States--History--Juvenile literature. I. Title.
 GV863.A1C435 2008
 796.357'646--dc22
                                    2007012110

Printed in the United States of America
1 2 3 4 5 6 7 8 9 0 11 10 09 08 07

Project Coordinator
James Duplacey

Design
Terry Paulhus

All of the Internet URLs given in the book were valid at the time of publication. However, due to the dynamic nature of the Internet, some addresses may have changed, or sites may have ceased to exist since publication. While the author and publisher regret any inconvenience this may cause readers, no responsibility for any such changes can be accepted by either the author or the publisher.

Every reasonable effort has been made to trace ownership and to obtain permission to reprint copyright material. The publishers would be pleased to have any errors or omissions brought to their attention so that they may be corrected in subsequent printings.

CONTENTS

What is the World Series?

The World Series is the baseball championship of Major League Baseball. Major League Baseball is made up of the American League and the National League. The World Series is played between the champions of the two leagues. The two teams play a best-of-seven series. The first team to win four games wins the series.

During the regular season, teams in each league play against each other. The best teams in each league get the chance to play in the World Series. The winner of the World Series is considered to be the best baseball team in the world.

The World Series is sometimes called the Fall Classic. This is because the series is played in the autumn. At first, the World Series was called the Championship of the World and the World's Championship Series. Over time, the name was shortened to the The World's Series and finally to the World Series.

Until the 1970s, most baseball players were from the United States. Since then, players from around the world have played Major League Baseball. Many have had the chance to play in the World Series. Players from Japan, Canada, Korea, South America, Australia, and the Dominican Republic have all played in the World Series.

Dave Roberts, a player for the Boston Red Sox, helped the Red Sox defeat the St. Louis Cardinals to win the 2004 World Series title.

The World Series is usually played in the United States. However, it has been played in Canada. The Toronto Blue Jays hosted World Series games in 1992 and 1993.

CHANGES THROUGHOUT THE YEARS	
PAST	**PRESENT**
Batters did not wear protection on their head, arms, or hands.	All batters must wear a helmet and often wear batting gloves, foot guards, and elbow pads.
All World Series games were played during the daytime.	All World Series games are played at night.
Each player on the winning team made $1,182.	Each winning player makes more than $360,000.
The World Series used two umpires.	The World Series now uses six umpires.

The World Series Trophy

The World Series trophy was created in 1967. It is 24 inches (61 centimeters) high, 11 inches (28 cm) wide, and weighs about 30 pounds (13.6 kilograms). The trophy is made of sterling silver, with 30 gold-plated flags that represent each Major League team. The flags surround a silver baseball.

The team that wins the World Series gets to keep the trophy. A new trophy is made every year. Players on the winning team get a World Series ring.

World Series History

The history of the World Series began with the formation of the National League. This league started in New York on St. Patrick's Day in 1870. Back then, it was called the National Association of Professional Base Ball Players and consisted of 10 teams. From 1884 to 1890, the champion of the National League played a series against the champion of the American Association (AA). The National League won five of the seven series that were played. The AA stopped playing in 1890. In 1901, a new league called the American League of Professional Baseball Clubs was formed. The league, which is sometimes called the junior circuit, had teams in eight cities. The two leagues became rivals. They competed for players and fans.

Willie Mays played in the World Series with Brooklyn, San Francisco, and the New York Mets.

The Boston Red Sox and the St. Louis Cardinals have played each other in the World Series three times. St. Louis won the series in 1946 and 1967. Boston won the championship in 2004.

In 1903, the National League and the American League decided to work together. They agreed to hold a championship series after the regular season was completed. The top team in the National League would play the top team in the American League. This is how the World Series began. The first World Series game was played between the Boston Pilgrims and the Pittsburgh Pirates at the Huntington Avenue Grounds in Boston. The Pilgrims won the series five games to three. The first **home run** in World Series history was hit by Pittsburgh's Jimmy Sebring.

There was no World Series in 1904. The National League champion New York Giants refused to play. Some fans thought they were afraid to lose to the American League. In 1905, the Giants won the National League title again. This time they agreed to play a series against Philadelphia. The Giants won the championship. The World Series has been played every year since 1903 except for 1994. A contract dispute between the players and the team owners stopped the season. The start of the 1989 World Series between Oakland and San Francisco was delayed for a week when an earthquake occurred on the California coast. The World Series has been played more than 100 times since 1903. The American League has won the most World Series titles.

Casey Stengel played with the Philadelphia Phillies before becoming a World Series-winning manager for the New York Yankees.

Baseball Mascots

The first baseball mascot was the San Diego Chicken. In 1974, a man named Ted Giannoulas was hired to dress as a giant chicken and hand out Easter eggs at a local zoo. His colorful costume made him very popular. The San Diego Padres baseball team hired him to entertain the fans. Soon, most major league baseball teams had a mascot.

Today, every major baseball team except the Los Angeles Dodgers and Chicago Cubs have a mascot.

Rules of the Game

Baseball was not always called baseball. The game has had several names, such as town ball, goal ball, rounders, and One O'Cat. There were many different rules. However, the basics of the game have always been the same. These are some of the most important rules that are used during a World Series baseball game.

1 The Game
There is no time clock in baseball. A World Series game is nine innings long. An inning lasts until three outs are made. If the game is tied, extra innings are played until there is a winner. Each team bats in an inning.

2 Winning the Game
Baseball is played between two teams of nine players. Each team tries to score more runs than the opponent. A run is scored when a player, or runner, steps on **home plate** after touching the three other **bases**.

3 The Pitcher
Pitchers must stand on the mound and have a foot on the rubber before they throw the ball to home plate. In American League parks, pitchers do not bat for themselves. A **designated hitter**, or DH, hits for the pitcher.

4 The Batter and the Bat
Batters must wear a helmet when they come up to the plate. In major league baseball, all bats must be made of wood. The bat cannot be more than 42 inches (107 cm) in length. It must be no more than 2.75 inches (6.9 cm) in diameter and made from one piece of solid wood.

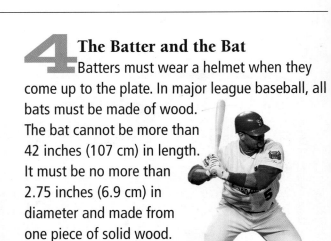

5 The Outs

A batter is out when three pitched **balls** go through the strike zone. The strike zone is as wide as home plate. It is as high as the distance between the batter's knees and the top of the batters belt. Batters are out if they hit the ball on the ground and the ball is thrown to first base before they reach the base. Batters are out if they hit the ball in the air and it is caught by a **fielder** before it goes into the stands.

CARDINALS			TONIGHT'S GAME
4	MOLINA	1B	AARON MILES
99	TAGUCHI	CF	2-FOR-4
16	DUNCAN	LF	GROUNDED OUT TWICE,
7	LUNA	SS	DOUBLED, SINGLED
19	PEREZ	RF	
26	SPIEZIO	3B	
53	RODRIGUEZ	DH	
28	BENNETT	C	BALL 0 STRIKE 0 OUT 0
12	MILES	2B	

	1 2 3	4 5 6	7 8 9	R	H	E	PITCHERS
CARDINALS	1 0 0	0 0 1	0 0 4	6	16	1	34 FLORES
WHITE SOX	0 0 11	2 0 6	1 0	20	24	0	65 MONTERO

6 Running the Bases

Batters that reach base are called runners. Runners must advance one base at a time and must touch second, third, and home plate for a run to be scored. Runners must try to advance if the ball is hit on the ground. If the ball is hit in the air, runners cannot leave their base until the ball is caught. At any time, runners can try to steal or move up a base without the ball being put in play. Runners who are tagged with the ball before reaching a base are out.

Making the Call

A regular season ball game uses four umpires. The World Series uses six umpires. The home plate umpire calls balls, **strikes**, outs, and **walks**. The first base umpire decides if the runner is safe or out. Second and third base umpires make calls at their base. There are two umpires in the **outfield**. They rule if a ball is fair or **foul** and if a catch has been made. Every umpiring team or crew has a crew chief. The crew chief has the final say on all rulings.

The Playing Field

The playing field in baseball has two parts, the **infield** and the outfield. This area is known as fair territory. The infield is the same size in every ballpark. The size of the outfield is different in most ballparks. There are no official rules about the size of the outfield. This is because the first baseball parks were often built in the middle of the city. There was not much room to build big parks. The outfield was made to fit the size of the space where the park was built.

The infield is shaped like a diamond. There are three bases and one home plate. Home plate is a five-sided, white rubber slab. This is where the batter, catcher, and umpire are positioned. On each side of the plate is an area called the batter's box. This is where the batter stands. Behind home plate is the catcher and umpire box. It is the same size as the batter's box. This is where the catcher and umpire are placed during a game. The catcher sits or squats behind home plate. The home plate umpire stands behind the catcher.

There is three-sided box on each baseline. The base coaches stand there. They tell the runners when to run or when to stay on base. In the middle of the infield, there is a raised area called the mound. This is where the pitcher stands. On top of the mound, there is a piece of white wood or hard rubber called the pitching rubber. Pitchers must have a foot touching the rubber when they throw a pitch to the batter. This is called toeing the rubber.

The area outside the infield and outfield is called foul territory. A ball hit on the ground in foul territory is not in play. A foul ball hit into the air that is caught is ruled as an out.

Players on the Team

There are nine players on the field. The catcher tells the pitcher what kind of pitch to throw and catches the pitches. The first, second, and third basemen play near their base. The shortstop usually plays between second and third base. There are three outfielders. The left and right fielder cover their side of the outfield. Center fielders are usually the fastest outfielders. They have to cover the rest of the outfield.

THE BASEBALL DIAMOND

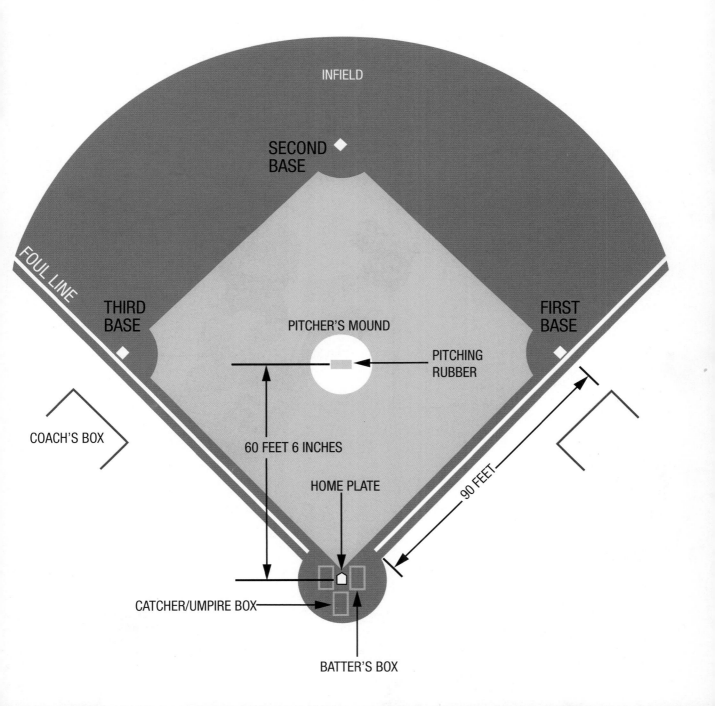

Baseball Equipment

Baseball is a simple game. The pitcher throws the ball, the batter hits the ball, and the fielders catch the ball. To play the game, most people only need a ball, a bat, and a baseball glove. Sometimes, catchers need extra equipment.

The size of a baseball has stayed the same since 1876. The ball was made from cowhide and often lasted the entire game. Today, most balls are made of cotton and yarn tightly wound around a rubber ball that is the size of a golf ball. The cover of a baseball is sewn on by hand. Big league baseball bats have not changed much over the years. They are made from solid pieces of wood, such as hickory or oak.

Until 1885, most players caught the ball with their bare hands. Now, they wear baseball gloves. There are special gloves for different positions.

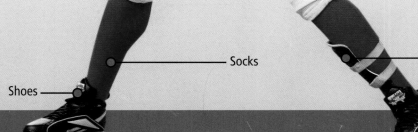

Bat

Helmet

Jersey

Batting gloves

GET CONNECTED

For a complete history of baseball equipment, visit 19th Century Baseball's website at **www.19cbaseball. com/equipment.html**.

Socks

Shin guard

Shoes

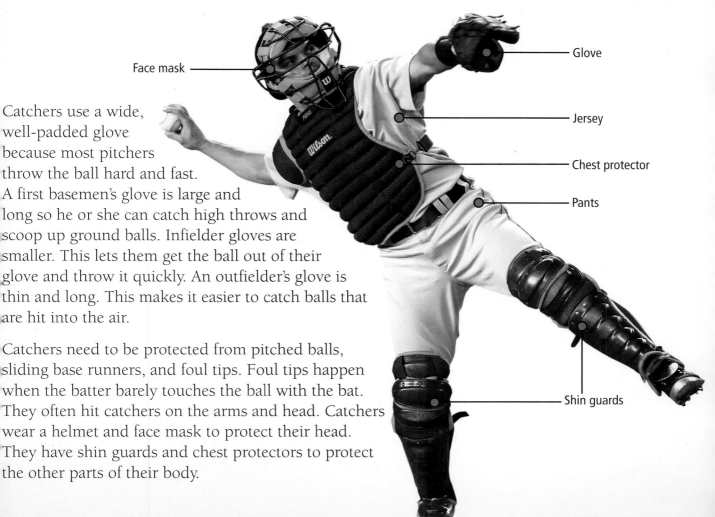

Face mask

Glove

Jersey

Chest protector

Pants

Shin guards

Catchers use a wide, well-padded glove because most pitchers throw the ball hard and fast. A first basemen's glove is large and long so he or she can catch high throws and scoop up ground balls. Infielder gloves are smaller. This lets them get the ball out of their glove and throw it quickly. An outfielder's glove is thin and long. This makes it easier to catch balls that are hit into the air.

Catchers need to be protected from pitched balls, sliding base runners, and foul tips. Foul tips happen when the batter barely touches the ball with the bat. They often hit catchers on the arms and head. Catchers wear a helmet and face mask to protect their head. They have shin guards and chest protectors to protect the other parts of their body.

Team Uniforms

Players usually wear the same uniforms in the World Series that they wear in the regular season. Some teams have worn special uniforms in the World Series. In 1905, the New York Giants wore black uniforms with white trim. The Chicago White Sox wore red, white, and blue uniforms in the 1917 World Series.

Today, every team that plays in the World Series wears a special shoulder patch on their uniforms. The patch marks their appearance in the Fall Classic.

Qualifying to Play

From 1903 until 1969, the only post-season baseball played was the World Series. There was no need for a playoff system. The winner of the National League pennant always played the winner of the American League pennant. If teams were tied after the regular season, another game or games were played to decide which team went on to to the World Series.

In 1969, Major League Baseball divided both leagues into two divisions, the East and West. The divisions played against each other to decide which team represented their league in the World Series. At first, this series was a best-of-five playoff. In 1985, the rules were changed. The Divisional Series became a best-of-seven round, like the World Series.

Four new teams were added to the Major Leagues in 1994. A new division, called the Central Division, was created in the American and National League. The three divisional winners advance to the playoffs.

The team with the best win-loss record that did not win a division is also allowed into the playoffs. Four teams from each league have the chance to make it to the World Series.

Flags standing on top of the scoreboard at Wrigley Field in Chicago show the standings in the National League's Central Division. The position of the flags on the flagpole are moved whenever there is a change in the standings.

The extra team is known as the wild card team. The wild card team must play all of their playoff games on the road. The only way they can get home field advantage is to advance to the World Series. The team with the home field advantage can play four games at home. This means it opens and closes the World Series in its own ballpark.

The home team in the World Series is decided in the All-Star Game. The All-Star Game is played in July. It is a game between the all-stars of the National League and the American League. The league that wins this game gets home field advantage in the World Series.

The All-Star Game gives players from different teams a chance to play together on the same team.

Wild Wild Cards

The first wild card team to make it to the World Series was the Florida Marlins. In 1998, they went on to defeat the Cleveland Indians and win the first World Series in team history.

In 2002, both teams that advanced to the World Series were wild card teams. The Anaheim Angels beat the San Francisco Giants to win their first World Series championship. Wild card teams won three straight World Series titles from 2002 to 2004. Anaheim, Florida, and the Boston Red Sox all won the World Series as wild card teams.

Where They Play

The outfield wall in Wrigley Field is covered with ivy through much of the season. A batter who hits a ball that becomes lost or caught in the vines is awarded second base. This is called a "ground rule" double.

In the early days, baseball was played in open fields. People could watch the game for free. Soon, players started getting paid to play. Team owners needed to raise money to pay the players. They built fences around the field and sold tickets. Fans who wanted to see the games had to pay to watch. The Union Grounds in Brooklyn, New York, was the first enclosed ballpark. It was built in 1862 and could seat 1,500 people.

Every baseball park is different. Some have unique features. Boston's Fenway Park has a 37-foot (11.2-m) high wall in left field. It is called the Green Monster. Houston's Minute Maid Park has an uphill slope in center field. Wrigley Field in Chicago has ivy covering its outfield walls.

Many teams build their ballparks to help their team. Yankee Stadium was designed so the team could hit could hit more home runs. The right field fence is only 312 feet (95 m) from home plate. The New York Yankees often hit more home runs than the other teams. It helped them win a record 26 World Series championships.

Bases used during World Series games have the official World Series logo stamped on them.

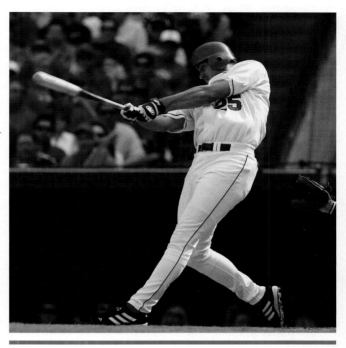

The field can be made to give an advantage to the home team. Some teams water down the dirt on the base paths. This makes it harder for runners to steal bases and helps teams with slow base runners. Teams that have fast runners sometimes let the grass on the infield grow longer. Balls hit on the ground take longer to reach the infielder. This helps the fast runners beat the throw to first base.

Teams can change the size of the foul territory in their park. This helps teams with pitchers that give up more fly balls than ground balls. Balls that are caught in foul territory are outs.

Troy Glaus hit three home runs in the 2002 World Series to help the Anaheim Angels win their first championship.

World Series Winners and Most Valuable Players 1997–2006

YEAR	WINNING TEAM	LOSING TEAM	WORLD SERIES MOST VALUABLE PLAYER
1997	Florida Marlins (NL)	Cleveland Indians	Levan Hernandez – Florida Marlins
1998	New York Yankees (AL)	San Diego Padres	Scott Brocius – New York Yankees
1999	New York Yankees (AL)	Atlanta Braves	Mariano Rivera – New York Yankees
2000	New York Yankees (AL)	New York Mets	Derek Jeter – New York Yankees
2001	Arizona Diamondbacks (NL)	New York Yankees	Randy Johnson/Curt Schilling – Arizona Diamondbacks
2002	Anaheim Angels (AL)	San Francisco Giants	Troy Glaus – Anaheim Angels
2003	Florida Marlins (NL)	New York Yankees	Josh Beckett – Florida Marlins
2004	Boston Red Sox (AL)	St. Louis Cardinals	Manny Ramirez – Boston Red Sox
2005	Chicago White Sox (AL)	Houston Astros	Jermaine Dye – Chicago White Sox
2006	St. Louis Cardinals (NL)	Detroit Tigers	David Eckstein – St. Louis Cardinals

Mapping the World Series

Roger Clemens

NORTH AMERICA

NORTH AMERICA

Freddie Garcia

SOUTH AMERICA

PACIFIC OCEAN

ATLANTIC OCEAN

SOUTH AMERICA

SOUTHERN OCEAN

Baseball players from around the world have played in the World Series. This map shows six of these players and where they were born. There has never been a Major League Baseball player born in Africa.

MAJOR LEAGUE BASEBALL PLAYERS BY CONTINENT 1870–2007

- AFRICA – 0
- ASIA - 68
- AUSTRALIA - 20
- EUROPE - 149
- NORTH AMERICA - 15,912
- SOUTH AMERICA - 213

Scale

621 Miles

0   1,000 Kilometers

Bert Blyleven
EUROPE

EUROPE

Bruce Bochy
EUROPE

Byung-Hyun Kim
ASIA

ASIA

PACIFIC OCEAN

AFRICA

INDIAN OCEAN

Graeme Lloyd
AUSTRALIA

AUSTRALIA

Women and Baseball

Women have been playing baseball since the game was invented. One of the earliest women baseball teams was started at Vassar College in 1876. Women from other colleges began to form their own teams. Soon, more women began to play the sport. Teams and leagues were created, and championship series were held.

Women have been competing against men's teams for many years. A team called the Franklin's Young Ladies Baseball Club Number 1 played in the 1880s. They often beat the men's teams they played against.

In Ohio, Alta Weiss became a star pitcher for a semi-professional men's team at the age of 17. Her father built a gym in the family barn so she could practice in the winter. In addition to playing baseball well, she was an excellent student. She became one of the first women to go to medical school.

Mildred Ella "Babe" Didrikson is often regarded as one of the best female baseball players of all time. She was so good, she pitched for the St. Louis Cardinals in an exhibition game against the Philadelphia Athletics.

GET CONNECTED

The American Women's Baseball Federation website has information about women's baseball, clinics, players, and tournaments. Go to **www.awbf.org**.

Victoria Brucker was the first girl to play in the Little League World Series, a 10-day tournament featuring the best 10- and 11-year-old players in the world.

Mamie "Peanut" Johnson played professional baseball in a man's league. She was a pitcher for the Indianapolis Clowns. She had a career record of 38 wins and eight losses. Johnson played with Henry Aaron, the first player to hit more than 700 home runs in the major leagues.

Two other women played in the same league as Johnson. Toni Stone played second base for Indianapolis and Kansas City. Connie Morgan played second base for Indianapolis after Stone was traded to Kansas City.

The Western Bloomer Baseball Club was a team of women who played exhibition games around the United States in the early 1900s.

The first Women's World Cup of Baseball was played in 2004. Teams from Australia, Canada, Japan, Taiwan, and the United States played in the event. The United States defeated Japan to win the gold medal. Japan captured the silver medal, while Canada won the bronze medal.

Women's Professional Baseball

In 1943, the Wrigley Gum Company started the All-American Girls Softball League. Soon, women were playing with the same size of baseball and the same rules that were used in Major League Baseball. The women's game became quite popular and helped raise the spirit of the country during World War II. The women did more than play baseball. They visited hospitals and raised money to help buy supplies for the war effort. The league played between 1943 and 1954. The story of the league and its players was told in the movie "A League of Their Own." The movie starred Tom Hanks and Madonna.

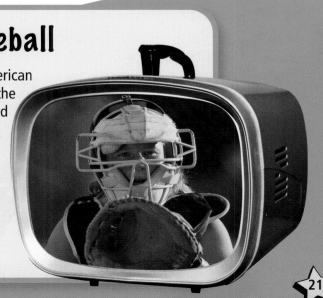

Historical Highlights

The New York Yankees have won the World Series 26 times. This is the most championships in the history of professional sports. The Philadelphia/Oakland Athletics are second to the Yankees. The team has won the World Series title nine times.

In 1960, Pittsburgh's Bill Mazeroski hit the first series-winning home run. This happened in the bottom of the ninth inning of the seventh game. Pittsburgh beat the New York Yankees to win the World Series.

Kirk Gibson of the Los Angeles Dodgers was not expected to play in the 1988 World Series. He had a badly injured leg and could barely walk. Still, he hit a home run in the bottom of the ninth inning in game one. His hit gave the Dodgers a win over the Oakland Athletics. It was the only time he played in the series.

Don Larson is the only pitcher in World Series history to pitch a perfect game. In game five of the 1956 World Series, he did not allow a single batter to reach first base in the entire game.

New York Giants outfielder Willie Mays made a game-saving catch to help lead his team to victory in 1954. He caught the ball over his shoulder. It is often referred to as the greatest catch ever made in the game of baseball.

In 1986, the Boston Red Sox were one out away from winning the World Series. Then, Boston first baseman Bill Buckner misplayed a ground ball. The ball went through his legs. His **error** allowed the New York Mets to win the game. They went on win the series.

Kirk Gibson is one of only seven players to hit a home run in the World Series for both a National League team and an American League team.

Joe Carter of the Toronto Blue Jays became only the second player to win a World Series with a home run in the last inning. He did it in game six of the 1993 World Series.

Babe Ruth is the only player to hit three home runs in a World Series game more than once. He did it in the 1926 and the 1928 World Series.

In 2002, Florida **rookie** Josh Beckett was named the World Series' most valuable player. He pitched a 2–0 shutout in game six to defeat the New York Yankees.

Yogi Berra played in the World Series both as a catcher and an outfielder for the New York Yankees.

WORLD SERIES RECORDS

WORLD SERIES RECORD	PLAYER(S)	TEAM
Most World Series championships (player) – 18	Yogi Berra	New York Yankees
Most consecutive base hits in one World Series – 14	Billy Hatcher	Cincinnati Reds
Most runs batted in, one World Series – 12	Bobby Richardson	New York Yankees
Most runs batted in, one World Series game – 6	Bobby Richardson	New York Yankees
Most strikeouts (batter) in one World Series – 12	Willie Wilson	Kansas City Royals
Most strikeouts (batter) in a World Series game – 5	George Pipgrass	New York Yankees
Most strikeouts (pitcher) in a World Series game – 17	Bob Gibson	St. Louis Cardinals
Most home runs in one World Series – 5	Reggie Jackson	New York Yankees
Most home runs in a World Series game – 3	Babe Ruth/Reggie Jackson	New York Yankees
Most World Series home runs (career) – 18	Mickey Mantle	New York Yankees
Most World Series hits (career) – 71	Yogi Berra	New York Yankees
Most World Series wins by a pitcher (career) – 10	Whitey Ford	New York Yankees
Most World Series saves by a pitcher (career) – 7	Mariano Rivera	New York Yankees

LEGENDS
and Current Stars

Curt Schilling

George Herman (Babe) Ruth –
Boston Red Sox, New York Yankees, Boston Braves

Babe Ruth is the only player to win the World Series as a pitcher and a fielder. He was a top pitcher and one of baseball's finest hitters. Ruth won three World Series games as a pitcher with the Boston Red Sox. He helped the team win the World Series in 1916 and 1918.

In 1920, Ruth was sold to the New York Yankees for more than $100,000. Ruth was such a good hitter that he became an outfielder so he could play every day. Ruth hit 15 home runs in World Series play. He helped lead the Yankees to four World Series titles.

Curt Schilling – Baltimore, Houston, Philadelphia, Arizona, Boston Red Sox

Curt Schilling has pitched in the World Series with three different teams. He helped the Philadelphia Phillies make the World Series in 1993. He pitched a 2–0 shutout in game five of that series.

In 2000, Schilling was traded to the Arizona Diamondbacks. He won 20 games in a season twice while he was with the team. In 2001, Schilling helped the Diamondbacks win the World Series. He shared the World Series' most valuable player (MVP) Award with teammate Randy Johnson. Following the 2003 season, Schilling was traded to Boston. In his first year with the Red Sox, he won 21 games. In 2005, Schilling helped the team win its first World Series title since 1918.

Babe Ruth

Reggie Jackson

Reggie Jackson – Kansas City/Oakland, Baltimore, New York Yankees, California

Reggie Jackson is known as Mr. October. This is because he hit 18 playoff home runs in October during his career. Jackson won three World Series titles when he played for the Oakland Athletics.

In 1977, Jackson signed with the New York Yankees. He led the team to back-to-back World Series wins. In the 1978 World Series, he hit a home run in four straight times-at-bat. No other player has ever been able to do this.

Jackson was the first player to hit 100 or more home runs for three different teams. He did it with Oakland, the New York Yankees, and the California Angels.

Derek Jeter – New York Yankees

Derek Jeter has played his entire career with the New York Yankees. He has helped the team win the World Series four times. Jeter did not miss the playoffs in his first 11 seasons in the major leagues. No other player in the history of major league baseball can match this accomplishment. Jeter has played in 119 playoff games. His career **batting average** in those games is 0.314, with 16 stolen bases and 17 home runs.

During his career, Jeter has won the Rookie of the Year and the All-Star Game most valuable player awards. He was named the World Series MVP in 2000. Jeter has won three gold gloves. These are awarded to the top defensive players in baseball.

Derek Jeter

Famous Firsts

The first World Series game played at night was between the Pittsburgh Pirates and the Baltimore Orioles on October 13, 1971. Pittsburgh won the game 4–3.

On October 20, 1992, the first World Series game outside the United States was played at the SkyDome in Toronto, Ontario, Canada. The Toronto Blue Jays defeated the Atlanta Braves 3–2. Toronto went on to win the World Series in six games. The Blue Jays won the World Series again in 1993.

Joe Carter's home run in the ninth inning of game six won the 1993 World Series for the Toronto Blue Jays.

In 1921, the World Series was broadcast on the radio for the first time. Grantland Rice, a sports writer and author, described the action for the fans listening to the games.

The first indoor World Series game was played on October 17, 1987, at the Hubert H. Humphrey Metrodome in Minneapolis. The Minnesota Twins defeated the St. Louis Cardinals 10–1.

The first "subway" World Series occurred in 1923. The New York Yankees once shared a ballpark with the New York Giants. In 1923, the Yankees moved to the new Yankee Stadium. When the Yankees and the Giants met in the World Series, it was called a subway series because fans could get to the games in both stadiums by taking the subway.

The 2000 World Series between the New York Yankees and the New York Mets was the first subway series since 1956.

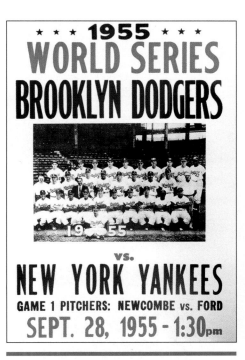

In the 1955 World Series, Brooklyn Dodgers' pitcher Johnny Podres had two complete-game victories. This means he pitched the entire game. He was the first player to be named as the most valuable player of the World Series.

Boog Powell was the first Major League Baseball player to play in the Little League World Series and the Major League World Series. He played in the Little League series with Lakeland, Florida, in 1954 and the World Series with the Baltimore Orioles in 1966.

The Philadelphia Phillies won the first World Series title in their 98-year history in 1980. They defeated the Kansas City Royals.

On October 12, 1982, Paul Molitor of the Milwaukee Brewers became the first player to have five base hits in a World Series game. He did it against the St. Louis Cardinals in game one of the series.

The first umpires to call a World Series game were Tom Connolly and Hank O'Day. The game was played at the Huntington Avenue Baseball Grounds in Boston on October 1, 1903.

The New York Yankees and the Brooklyn Dodgers played in the 1955 World Series. It was the fifth World Series meeting in nine years between the two clubs.

The Yankees Dynasty

A dynasty is a team that has won three championships in a row or four in six years. The New York Yankees have had many dynasties. The first was from 1921 to 1928. During this time, the Yankees won the World Series three times. The second dynasty was from 1936 to 1941, when they won five World Series titles. From 1947 to 1964, the Yankees won ten championships. The latest dynasty went from 1996 to 2001. They won the Series five times.

The Rise of the World Series

1845

The Knickerbocker Base Ball Club forms in New York. It publishes the first rules of what will become modern-day baseball.

1903

The first World Series game takes place between Pittsburgh and Boston at the Huntington Avenue Baseball Grounds.

1910

The Star Spangled Banner is played for the first time during a World Series game.

1924

Walter Johnson helps the Washington Senators beat the New York Giants.

1943

The Wrigley Gum Company forms the All-American Girls Softball League.

1947

Jackie Robinson becomes the first African American to play in the World Series.

1968

Bob Gibson of the St. Louis Cardinals strikes out 17 Detroit Tigers.

2004

The Boston Red Sox win their first World Series championship since 1918 by defeating the St. Louis Cardinals in four straight games.

2001

The Arizona Diamondbacks beat the New York Yankees in six games. Josh Beckett wins the final game with a 2–0 shutout.

2002

Tsuyoshi Shinjo becomes the first Japanese player to play in a World Series game.

1977

Reggie Jackson hits three home runs in game six of the World Series.

1989

An earthquake in California postpones the start of the World Series between San Francisco and Oakland.

1991

Minnesota Twins' Jack Morris pitches a 10-inning shutout against the Atlanta Braves in game seven of the World Series.

QUICK FACTS

- A World Series record crowd of 92,706 fans watched the Los Angeles Dodgers defeat the Chicago White Sox 5–4 on October 6, 1959.

- In 1920, Bill Wambsganss turned the only unassisted triple play in World Series history. He recorded all three outs in an inning on the same play. Wambsganss caught a line drive for one out and touched second base for the second out. Then, he tagged the runner coming from first base for the triple play.

- The Huntington Avenue Grounds was torn down in 1911. It is the now the site of Northeastern University in Boston, Massachusetts.

Test Your Knowledge

1 How many home runs did Babe Ruth hit in the World Series?

2 What was the name of the ballpark where the first World Series game was played?

3 How many umpires work in a World Series game?

4 What was the name of the first baseball mascot?

5 What is the nickname of the wall in Fenway Park?

6 Whose home run ended the 1960 World Series?

7 What player was nicknamed "Mr. October"?

8 Who pitched the only perfect game in World Series history?

9 What woman once pitched in an exhibition baseball game?

10 What team has won the most World Series titles?

Further Research

Many books and websites provide information on the World Series. To learn more about the championship of Major League Baseball, borrow books from the library, or surf the Internet.

Books to Read

Most libraries have computers that connect to a database for researching information. If you input a key word, you will be provided with a list of books in the library that contain information on that topic. Non-fiction books are arranged numerically, using their call number. Fiction books are organized alphabetically by the author's last name.

Online Sites

For information about Major League Baseball teams and games, visit **http://mlb.com**.

Baseball Almanac has information about the history of the sport at **www.baseball-almanac.com**.

For online activities, facts, and videos, check out Major League Baseball for Kids at **www.mlb.com/mlb/kids**.

Glossary

balls: pitches that a batter does not swing at and does not pass through the strike zone

bases: square canvas sacks that cover three points of the baseball diamond in the infield

batting average: base hits divided by number of times at bat

designated hitter: a player who hits for the pitcher in the American League

error: misplaying a batted ball or making a poor throw that results in a player advancing on the base paths

fielder: a player who is on the infield or in the outfield

foul: a ball that is hit outside the field of play

home plate: a five-sided slab of rubber or wood that helps establish the strike zone

home run: a ball hit in fair territory that allows the batter to run around the bases and score a run

infield: the area of the baseball field where the bases, mound, and home plate is located

outfield: the area of a baseball field between the diamond and the home run fence

rookie: a player in his first season

strikes: pitches the batter swings at but misses, foul balls, or balls that pass through the strike zone

walks: reaching first base after four pitched balls miss the strike zone

Index